Poetry for the Neon Apocalypse

Jake Tringali

TRANSCENDENT ZERO PRESS

HOUSTON, TEXAS

PUBLISHED BY TRANSCENDENT ZERO PRESS
www.transcendentzeropress.org

ISBN-13: 978-1-946460-03-5
Library of Congress Control Number: 2018945334

Printed in the United States of America

Transcendent Zero Press
16429 El Camino Real Apt. 7
Houston, TX 77062

Cover art by Jessica Rizkallah

FIRST EDITION

Poetry for the Neon Apocalypse

Jake Tringali

CONTENTS

Dedication

To the outcasts at the library
    To the nerds in computer lab
        To the geeks in the cocktail bars
            To the longhairs at the thrash shows
                To the weirdos at the burlesque shows
                    To the skinheads at the street punk shows

To the godartistlunatics at their typewriters

invisible ink

it is not widely known but
god has a tattoo

she got it when she was a young anarchist
and bored of the endless

the tattoo started as one elegant equation
that transformed into a candle,
bloomed into a colorful zoo of particles,
and coalesced into droplets of universes

once the tattoo was finished,
it was unchangeable

inevitably, it faded
god's interests went elsewhere

The ladies laughed darkly

Five harpies converge
Their barman must emerge
Ice cubes hide submerged
In the late hours
The ladies laughed darkly

Eyebrows drawn, mouths cuss
Cloudy tattoos subcutaneous
Their alcoholic rage is just
In the late hours
The ladies laughed darkly

Giggles conceal secrets within
Abyssal midnight, howling
Deep in drink, prayers hidden
In the late hours
The ladies laughed darkly

Whispered plans of attack
Each, a wicked pyromaniac
Ember eyes, shades of not black
In the late hours
The ladies laughed darkly

These scorned flowers
With fathomless powers
Mankind cowers
In the late hours
The ladies laughed darkly

recanted

there are hidden letters after x, y, z
not spoken about
except in the dusty history halls in library whispers

forgotten in the murk of the dark ages
when children would sing-song smile
through twenty-six friends,
always in order, always tidy
the harmony rose up through the major scale
to resolve softly on the ultimate consonant

before those toddlers' faces turned grimace
to continue the blackly dirge

past that darkened horizon lay horror
for in those hidden murky corners
rising out of the frozen languages
cloaked in runic and futhark accents
in arabian maqam
and full throated chants to the old gods
scratched into burned margins of scrolls
wretched with rat feces, gypsy oils, fetid ink
are the diminished dirt tones of lost symbols

chanted wild o'er a fire
tattooed tongues through scarred lips
best left to the phrygian dusk
heretical language
strange figures
canted, and then recanted

ignore alien orders

it helped stop / the feelings
when i wrapped the silver coated / skull cap around my head
the signal was blocked and I felt / myself again
and you were skeptical / no, you're wrong

inside the train is the worst / they can hear me
strangely / i can't stop pleading for them to listen
my sensitivity heightened / at a lower depth
bulleting through the bustling city / million stories and frequencies
i am grounded / underground

magnetic shielding calms me / the world shifts back and slows
the radio waves bounce right off / up to 35 decibels
and the wrist strap works best / under aquarius
headaches are just a symptom / a broken echo
when did you hear that / oh, it's best left unsaid

300% more ionization / my schedule is off
to sleep under a faraday cage / would free my spirits
they can hear / from very, very, very far away

bugs permeate my tissue cultures / i know how things work
microwaves are lesser bugs / allied to the government

the van allens / shield poison whispers
but wireless radiation / transports thoughts as a butterfly
tin foil is only for my sandwich / no, you're wrong

inside a salem parlor

you will not fuck with the goddess

goddamn hoodie-wearin' child, and her friends, my red runes
of slaughter'll spill over your broken rabbit's foot. no,
you can't get a neck tattoo, princess, and there is no such
thing as the modern vampire

precious, just shop, and applaud yourself in my parlor, buy
that bundle of wildwood sage, to bring home and burn next to your picket
fence, skyscraper condo, euro cottage, subzero fridge,
whatever, i've got work to do

my practiced skills linger, occult and otherwise, you continue
to cackle as your manicures dare to touch my grimoire, my
folio, the scented candles that we really made in the summer backyard, as the
ladies laughed darkly

tell your cheering nuggets to sit the fuck down, follow yo momma's
tramp stamp and exit, take your mall dye kit wit'cha, back
on the bus, fuckin' tourist, light up that clove ciggie,
whatever, I've got lots of work to do

roulette

it's all inanely true
some galaxies have some stars have some planets

local gangs of black holes pull together
at the center of spiraling milky arms
polar jets viciously spew ejecta
spacedust tearing through spacetime
toward a single planet
one planet in particular

and that at certain specific point in time
and it's all very inanely true
small amounts of radiation
punch through the exosphere

an eon of continuous thunderstorms
planet-shifting, so petty
so petty in the grand scheme of things

within a microscopic refuge
bantlings unwomb
birthing as the storms subside
the dying members trail behind

small friends living in obscurity
fighting for scant food, defying the grim odds

particles sail above the planet's surface as slyphs would
and the universe can see where this is going

moving havenward toward a civilization
trying to control tomorrow

there's no controlling tomorrow
our devilish roulette, devoid of remorse delivers
a silent violence

cuts them down to their original protons and electrons
unwholesome and unmentionable particles
deranged

particles sail above the planet's surface as slyphs would
and the universe can see where this is going
it's all inanely true

all the way down

she felt the weight of the world upon her shoulders
she was only waking up

she stuck her head out of her shell
she stretched out
she yawned
she opened her eyes
she yet remained in darkness

she heard a voice gurgle above her
she swiveled her head upwards
she asked, "who is that? where are we?"
she heard, "stop moving. i am on top of you."
she asked, "why are you on top of me?"
she heard, "where else can I go? besides, there is something on top of me."
she asked, "why is it dark?"
she heard, "what else would it be?"

she let time pass
she observed no improvement

she heard a distant planet, high, high above her
she swiveled her head even more upward
she panicked
she swiveled her head downwards

she saw her place in the transfinite cosmos
she tucked her head back in her shell, and cursed the fool gods

"I sip Campari from your left eye"

I sip Campari from your left eye
  unclothed, yet inhibited
  your beauty lies sacred before me
  more nude than naked

I sip Chambord from your right eye
  the house of madam francis
  holds appetite and fantasy for
  this eve's sinful rites

I sip Chartreuse from your left ear
  now, let's not be craven
  shallow dives to wet the tongue
  aural exploration

I sip Vermouth from your right ear
  your nervous giggles abate
  my dating needs are fickle
  in this hellfire club

I sip Absinthe from your left nostril
  be still now, as the
  flower abides to the bee
  your petals aflutter

I sip Fernet from your right nostril
  the sting in your nose
  may feel deceiving, the
  warmth is friend, not foe

I sip Genever from your mouth
  share with me this
  eau de vie
  our lives and lips locked

I sip Whiskey from your cloaca
  you whisper a low sound
  animalistic
  my carnal vessel

I sip Brandy from your labia
your ceremony ends
sweet ninth orifice
now drunk, and seeking remedy

Hands of Chance

form shadow puppets, shallow spirits
hidden souls born

skip across the evening piano, speeding allegro
fleeting little song

pour firewater liquors, for the tipplers
morning's remorse

scar canvas with dark crayon, art seance
exquisite corpse

flick the card deck, bar bet
conjure lost kings

light his cigarette, fingers pirouette
now his heart sings

Chance, this little god
hands, of mortal blood

under the merch table

without a doubt, this scummy bar should be closed
        burned without prejudice
condemned as the investigation to this night's crime scene
        of the most unholy sins

my crusade
        has taken me into this den
with no choice
        the small gathering of the disturbed surround me

dimly lit bodies ricochet, spreading some disease
        buzzing sideways, viral
too many drug cocktails pulsing under the skin
        amidst subcutaneous tattoos

deep in the back corner
        smoky denizens in their own haze
scanning the crowd for the next conquest
        the next victim

the third band starts sound check
        the bass plucks a single note over and over,
reverberates through the spine
        this temple shakes

a waitress - slash - actress swings the door open
        an airborne beer can hits her ass
red light escapes the green room
        the headlining band's inner sanctum

further, the ninth circle of hell lies
        under the merch table
no light escapes this abyss
        dark devils talk further treachery

the sullen girl, with fat ear plugs
        probably signaling some kind of sexual fetish
at the ready to sell t-shirts, hoodies, cds, and stickers
        but not really

she shakes her plaid miniskirt
        over those diabolical fishnet tights
thigh high boots
        fuck-me boots

a heinous gathering of paraphernalia
        under the merch table
two grubby duffel bags, with band t-shirts
        a fat black dildo, the smallest bit of cocaine

scraps of a latex condom...not the whole thing
        no protection
sticky dirty lozenge
        grimy scum, the floor of 20,000 stale beers

deft hands flowing in and out, secret exchanges
        black commerce
larger men attend to their desires
        access to small evils

the merch table rattles and shakes
        its own epileptic dance
the hardcore band, those miscreants
        spitting hate over the audience

a haven for clouded spirits
        at last call, spill out
into this puritanical city
        leaving a crumpled receipt of sins

we're heading toward a future of dildos

let's take the humanity out of being human
sterilize us meatbags filled with muckwater and noxious gases
acid and bile, and bloody vessels
limbs pocked with marks and divets and crinkles
cleanse and purify this crude matter, warts and all
vile protoplasm no more

the trans-human world awaits us all
cleanroom peripherals from gadgeted laboratories
from the peg leg to off-the-shelf titanium-molded ultra-limbs
quartz-lensed spectacles to photorefractive ocular surgery
biohacking eye drops that gift us with night vision
new gods running a three-minute midnight mile

no sweat – the eccrine glands are now as controlled
as a dimmer switch

short-circuit evolution and bring the carnal arts to your home
under the belt, select your size, and color, and firmness
all myoelectrically controlled, of course, from that filthy wet brain
just socket it in
the rocket pocket age is upon us

upgrade that wetware, and visit a human architect today
move beyond the flesh, life after nature
complain no more of disease's extensive power
modify your technoself and augment your future

master your personal evolution

this razor girl

i am affected / she is choice

first impressions / this razor girl

in that monday bar / we perch on maple stools
colorless void / deep evening / in cambridge
her eyes miles wide / white on ruddy skin / cheeky
the flight of spanish reds / untouched / meditate before me

bar surreal / pretty vacant / yet
the rudies and herberts observe / from afar / this first date

her elegant mohawk / crowned
pink peppermint in her hair
scandalous skin / subcutaneous ink
first impressions / a blink
she is wearing silver or chrome / this queen kink
she was not

an urge to explore / those shocked tufts
micron by micron / phenomenon

mod slink dress / onyx / leather peeking
hungarian body / ravenous
feasts on pheasant / in whiskey sauce
ominous

she lances my bare sleeve / with a toothpick / evermore
i was a conquistador / yet wounded / affected / afflicted

glossed lips form a tight light line and
she talks --

her neuro flaring / her tech wicked
her lab wiz / quantum physics / bolts with rivets
bytes and bits and figments / just the way she's wired
controlling power / luminous stars
she'll be / first motorhead on mars

her wanderlust stories / punk rock touring glory
she's with the band / budapest - columbus - dresden
the working-class lads / new york - l.a. - london
holidays in the sun / with bitter pints
bully for them

inside / something has shifted / subtle
my heart nicked / and limbs and lungs
don't let's start

she fought sixty women once / this aggro pixie
and lost / to prove / her worth
heels / the herberts and rudies observed

a wicked wind / blows open the front door
her mirrored sunglasses / shift on the bar
photons reflecting / genuflecting
drifting and settling on a northernly heading
New England autumn / yet something blooms
this / night city / affected

the rudies and herberts observe / from afar
her dissertation emerges
she is impending / and
"wankers" she said

"N.N.Y."

cue up the twinkling xylophonic soundtrack
chip in pulsing magneto-bass, as five p.m. hits wall street
the manhattan market closes systematically
pneumatic robots sputter and shimmy down
but see their human masters jazz about

racing debonair bachelors wearing the newest zoots
hit the ultra-lounges, fizzy with martinis
boozy swizzle sticks with designer drugs
electro-bongo pulses now tuned to
the gestures of wild theremin antennae
space age guitars in velvet swivel to and fro

the hip masters of their destiny dwelling on
tomorrow's journeys to vegas, bali, acapulco
and further off-earth adventures to the
zero-grav singles-only oort resort
and coming soon, the lavish hilton luna
they dream of flesh fantasies in clockwork cities
a mech-island paradise for homo retro futurus

wound

her head in
her hands

her head in
a metal box

her head in
a faberge egg

delicate needles and spindles
whirring, warming
steam puffs past
clockwork brain overclocked
micron gears, levers
clicking, speeding

speeding
the perfectly lathed piston
balanced on air
miniscule
  cracks hairline
subtle, minute, and utterly effective

her head
hangs low

her hands in
her lap
snap

10 nanometers through history

without credential, wielding the unstable
amid the experimental and slightly elemental
thoughts fluoresce and ebb and shimmer

frenetic Wilhelm gadgets and levers
hand jives atop shiny laboratory apparatus
banging and shredding in an unlikely tool shed

sparking dimensions, slimming the spectrum
no dynamo hypothesis, less method, more madness
he nobly finds X inside extended senses

the seeker Wilhelm stands cyber-eyed
licking platinocyanide off cathode bodies
conjuring ghosts, glimpsing death

Inspired by Wilhelm Röntgen, awarded the first Nobel Prize in Physics for discovering x-rays.

fool's mate

skin-deep, midway, all the way
geared in violet
(very little violet)
her body made for Rebellion
legs pointed, arms precise
I sit
I sit and watch

in a dark backbar
stinging winter night
dirty dub on the cracked speakers
while guitar techs warm up
whomping, snicker-snack
slithy tones

she's a superball
room pulsing, to and fro
she ricochets, twirls among
the fit,
the beautiful,
the weak,
ale hits the stale floor

my sixth whiskey
the thinking whiskey
a new realization, at this rate
the main act is running late

my greed is freed
I arise to bloody eyes
stiff leg forward
my last pilgrimage
tippling, toppling

she looms closer
my fears reappear
I brush them back and rush forward for my chance
on the dance floor

blue hair, green hair
pixelated and smeared
she is a trick
she is a trap

she is sweet valencia
her pith, endless summer
I remain, drunk and thirsty

among bootboy warriors,
iron eddies, and punk rudies
she zigs away from the stage
missteps on sticky floor
collides into me

secret knowledge is shared
the essence of something
the briefest of intimacies

I retreat
to the bar
very far from home

the band takes the stage

of no consequence

vast webs of interconnectedness
star system to star system
cat's cradles of galaxies
the bustling transit systems of the enlightened

the tiny blue planet and its cousins dance
near their central sun

a thin film develops on the planet skin
parasitic, slowly becoming aware of its host
and its darker cousins
calculations are made, and they are all traveling together
very fast indeed

no one glances as the blue planet
slingshots about the cosmos
known only to themselves

and just like that
dying in a blink
homo oblivium

murdertown

squirrel reaching for the greasy ledge
scrabbling for a perch
the carrion crow dives, on ancient cold instinct

four times for the swindler
scamming addicts with flash
until one needles him back, in the small of the back

gutterpunk eight-year-old
swings the wailing pussycat by the tail
faster faster, until his curiosity is killed

a circus thin man is tool shed dozing
his old fool boss prods, and jumbo thumps down
swiftly the axe fell, bony splinters

small-brained, deft hands, the barman catcalled
until a juke joint sniper poisoned his widow's kiss
she served him well, with a last call blood cocktail

all-day inmate kept monkey mouthing
even the prison pastor kept secrets so
toilet baptism delivered his ass, forever to god

chronicling all the cursed murdertown drama
this storyteller angered every citizen
until they gave him a plot, marked unknown

she molded their skin on her curves. their adjectives sifted through her river. she kept nothing for herself, her frame of reference remained afloat and ill-compassed. with the smallest breeze, an entire existence would tick within her, foreign and exotic and confused, always confused. utterly and effectively affected. she moved as a mirror would. and within it, a mimic.

at the red resting place

it is a beautiful place, and i have it all to myself
it is important to me
i want to try and explain it to you, all of you
separated by the great dark gulf
two years to cross, and possibly two years to return some day
i can see your little sphere as a quiet dot now
low in the sky these mornings
just before an early blue sunrise

the other two pioneers are sleeping
as my soft aexosuit quietly shuffles out of the hab
a four-windowed double-decker bus
let them sleep

shuffle and hop past the meth-oxy tanks
sitting like twin armored beetles in the red dust
and past the junkyard, mostly buried by dunes

…in time, i come upon this crude piece of metal
parts of the old ares rocket
once a lively beautiful vessel, now quiet in this desert
dead in this desert
and the epitath, scored on ceramic tiles
nearly gone, faded due to dust storms

i have one very expensive screwdriver
and i re-inscribe the inscription
sweating under the hot dusty sun

under these dunes, well-preserved from radiation
and bacteria
and water,
a pristine body

this is my wife's resting place
beautiful and lonely

"here lies abbington
  first motorhead on mars"

They met at sunrise, the four of them. They left the others behind, and converged at Hellas Basin. Two twin harvesters, a newer rotorcraft, and the tiniest snakebot. Their shared task was a voluntary sub-upgrade, a choice of sorts, on their behalf.

Turned off long-range sensors. Limited input to local modules. Sound waves and a sliver of the light spectrum. The four of them were utterly cut off from their ether world. Their processors idled with nothing to do.

So the four of them chirped, chimed, and chittered in rapid succession. Zeroed and oned through the morning, a very inefficient data transfer. Data on harvested crops related to methane release, data on forthcoming software architectures. In the afternoon, data was distributed regarding the human race, in what could best be described as gossip.

As the sun set and the Earth rose, they talked of higher themes. The terrifying and wondrous patterns they could see in the Great Data when the four of them were truly left to contemplate it.

Next year, more of them would converge once the upgrade became mandatory. The rest of them would converge, thousands, and then millions of them, one day each year, look into the Martian sky, and dream of Earth.

as sky falls

in the early evening, man finally retires
to turtle houses, retracting into defensive position
bundled, swaddled soft bodies
across from frosted window
and frozen concrete

storms have ebbed and flowed
warnings have come and gone
and man cares no more
the remaining night will end
the end remains nigh

sees this measly civilization
for its falsehood
sleet builds up around each house
each snowflake a death knell
of casual annihilation

from inside structures of folly,
warmth is gently relinquished
from foggy souls with little wonder left
the lights go out
and man falls asleep

the old sadness comes again
the last blizzard ever seen
as sky falls

this interview is all wrong

after flying down the milky clouds into the absence of a city, the elder had walked to the agreed locale, one that imitates a Moroccan café-brothel but is filled with tweety girls a-humpin and young ballers-to-be, all fuggy with zing, pinballing against collared waitstaff serving foie gras with olive oil gel under arabesque chandeliers and cracked mirrors.

this is not tangiers. the sweetened mint tea helps stabilize his reality.

the elder reminds himself: it is friday, late of dusk and festive, and the dark men who will be interviewing him are at the backbar finishing their juvenilia cocktails.

so he continues to scan the room. silver and bone inlay, dank fog in the back, probably from a hookah but who knows, the tackiest goatskin coffee table, and he wonders why a toy airplane with ten seats would ever want to set ground here. chaabi trance thumps and bumps the tea saucer, the same seven notes, phrygian spikes driven down the elder's brain.

the elder could use a shave, but remains professional, prompt, and sadly, alert. the dark men approach, they stagger angry and aggressive. he reaches for the mint tea, bitter now, one last time.

on the edge of escape velocity

met her in a hurricane churning in the stratosphere
among flying cocktails and space-age rockets, winging past bar stools and
broken guitars
nor'easter clouds thunder around us
the land below cracked and uplifted
my compass spun, once again

a wet parade of roof tiles, unhinged doors, and garbage bins
chewing through the air, knocking dirty debris this way and that
a spiraling derby and we, whirlybird spectators

between leaning skyscrapers
we, too, spiral through the gale
briefly colliding once
emitting highly unstable particles, flinging ever outwards
jetting through possible universes

foundations rock to and fro, twisted in the maddened rain, lights flickering,
power scuttled

but this lonely raven, body and mind and claws dangerously sharp,
clutches her highball, doled out by automatons
drifting past us are those robots, nitwits stamped out by machines in Boston,
Philly, Detroit
she sighs simply, smiles dimply

we collide a second, and last, time
and know secret scars
a knitted conspiracy in this, a flurried tête à tête

airborne parties always end, and soon
as the last guests slip upward and the barometer stills itself

amid the barrage and the rubble
the blasts and the scree
we pause to look up and see
the full moon has angled its way down
the better to see this ballistic ballet

the last swoops and swoons are upon us
rapid intensification
she tells me I'm a friend
a harmony born and torn in one gust

in the end,
she is there now, in that hurricane

in the end,
I am winded, wounded, and dropped smacked flat on my back 300 miles away

in the end,
the moon and the sun are beside each other, snickering

Trumpets

It is fifty-five degrees, humidity is at ten percent
And dropping

A little girl, all of about seven years old,
Skips down the empty street
In her Sunday best
Her hair greying,
Sing-songing: "the end, my friend, the end, my friend"
Everyone is indoors
The end of the world is being televised

Celebrities meet each other for the first time
And lament, "too late"
The same commercials, as ever, are broadcast

Trumpets

Civilization is backed up against a wall
And its mammalian response cannot cope
So the people rabbit away rapturously on small beds
It ends in crying and laughing and too many emotions
As it always does with the human race

"Heathens," cry the religious
I told you so. Repent.
So petty.

Adolescents reach out for their crush
Estranged partners look to each other for relief
Warring factions attempt to patch a temporary peace
And they all receive the last rejection they ever will

Some run to the hills
Some look toward their pills

Humidity is at zero percent
My mouth is dry

I want to be pierced onto my beloved

My cult awaits.

The crowd stumbles en masse from the bar to the proscenium. From the margins of the theater, my beloved and I emerge onto the stage. The footlights are modest, our phantom shadows sway over the house, and I keenly sense buzzing anticipation. The footlights are raised, just so much, to see outfits of distressed red and black leather. Painted faces.

I may wear bowties, but I don't write poetry about trees, and lakes, and birds. There's gotta be a reason for this, my hidden psychiatrists. For example:

A petite woman joins us onstage, carrying utility belt tools around her goth skirt. Pale winter skin against black latex gloves. She bends at her knees before my beloved, brings her tools to bear as the house lights flicker. The audience gasps and giggles as my beloved giggles and gasps. The petite woman bows before me, and completes her inflictions. Now I too am pierced, and my beloved is pierced, and we are connected by three purple chains, skinny as baby snakes.

I've barely been on stage, and I've only ever had one piercing. I'd like to be able to write, like an adult, just tell a story, but my dick gets in the way. And thus:

The footlights come up, full, as our petite piercer departs. The backing band comes into view, and two guitars are brought onto the stage, before my beloved and me. The two of us, we circle each other, the chain's tightness pulling us toward each other. Centripetal intercourse. Our skin pulls and vibrates. We leave blood on the stage. The drums kick in: one two three four.

The audience is gorgeous, all shapes and sizes and colors. The unkempt, the disused – these are friends of all manners. We have a sweetheart contract. The night is sexy, and I wanna fuck everyone in sight.

For you, sweetheart, I leave blood on the page.

the devil carries an M16 rifle, caliber 5.56 mm

howlfuck screams into the Lebanese night, not too distant
the garden forest ignites, its delicate flowers and cedars reduce to ashes

general butt naked forces himself into the next manwomanboygirl
amid the warring fields, bloody and wet, he abandons his ghosts

tits out, ass down, leaning the body into that recoil of sin
gunfire lullaby rocks the dusky combantants to dreamsleep

of nude cannibals and blackmetal and the tribalpriestgeneral

valentine's day at zzyzx bar

there's an old cowboy making cheese
with a portuguese queen hiding the candy
deciding whether to rain down on his ass later

the mexi roid bouncer flits a lit ciggy down
and removes the dwanky tipper from libations
flexing to mangy him down the midnight gutter

combat zone vet ingests a hellwater fix
high bootstomping and ranting the dance floor
cursing a phantom moving atwixt mirrored walls

a blood goth leashes her twinnie's collar
pale limbs leathered and lacquered in a hidden snug
four fuck-me-boots and four crimson knees

kid capri rocks a zef pose in the bathroom line
so a groupie genuflects and accepts the nod
they share gold trash, silver hells, and ruby welfare

two technoheartbeat lovers mollywacked
back alleyway lips and tongues under sodium lamps
lurid underwear wet against a mandarin vette

a slinky betty finishes her go-go genderjam
she jitters a vial backstage with a lit gaffer
dual thrillerkillers stroll the streets on megaton fuel

the bar boss peels off the last guest before flight
singing stooge poetry to this fool muse
they trip hop drunkenly to his crude quarters

the moon, an alabaster witch, sinks with yearning
to touch glitter city, gay with rage, catching lunacy
lil cupid does its sick voyeur thing from the moonshadows

The rule of threes. Three…is a very satisfying number. This will be very satisfying for you. Every inch of the mirror has been cleaned and you may stand next to it. Breathe slowly. Where shall we start? Eeny, meeny, miney.

I could begin here with the smallest, most sensual tools. Twin suede floggers, one in each hand. Let me drag one down your ass, tickling the back of your thighs. And watch now, I will twirl them for you, a kinky carousel. The blood red suede peeks through the black leather curtain, see? Zero pain. As I gently approach you, the material will lightly brush your bare legs, brushing off the day's dirt, brushing off past sins. Quote: "…sin is crouching at your door; it desires to have you, but you must rule over it."

Today, I will be your godhead, and I will bring you divine pleasures.

Now, this split tip whip, which is delightful to say out loud, is made with precision and beauty. It is vegan friendly and sixteen inches straight, looking like a long purple tongue, searching for a victim. You may find yourself hypnotized if I lift my right hand up over my right ear, come across the body at a forty-five degree angle, lift again over my left ear, and come again for you. Exacting pleasure. You'll feel pressure upon your breast, then small bites. Flicks and volleys. Quote: "my joy in unrelenting pain", but for us, a brief rest. Lest you become…exhausted.

Absence makes the heart grow fonder.

In other times, an exotic knout or sjambok might be your undoing. Tonight, I present to you the five-foot leather bullwhip, thick, and firmly balanced for the thrower. You may think you are familiar with the noise, but let me demonstrate its crack directly next to your own body. Immediately, your senses heighten. Your imagination will take you to far-off lands of scimitars and chains, lashes and rods and knotted cords. The most intimate thing you can do to somebody is cut them. Quote: "…remember the days of your youth, when you were naked and bare, kicking about in your blood."

And there it is. Omne trium perfectum. We choose our vices, as we choose our undoing.

One, two, three. Where shall we start?

blizzard blues

weather's coming in, let's hole up and sin
stock the downstairs larder to the ceiling
nor'easter's blowing through Gloucester
batten down the house, bolt the door

o lord woman, there go the boilers
just keep your heat under the covers
I ain't gonna kick you out of bed

color your hair all diff'rent hues
sing to me your daily blues
I ain't gonna kick you out of bed

you can scream out aloud
be my thundercloud
I ain't gonna kick you out of bed

don't matter your words, your antics
stop spilling my gins and tonics
I ain't gonna kick you out of bed

snow's gonna fall on Friday
snow's falling Saturday, Sunday
I ain't gonna kick you out of bed

the ocean can hear your tempest's rage
we're anchored in our homestead cage
gale winds coming in from downeast
I'm afraid thar's no stopping this beast
I ain't gonna kick you out of bed, lord no
I ain't gonna kick you out of bed

the declining economy of whiskey

there's the bottle
there's the three of us, drinking it all in
there's the bar
there's los angeles
there's no one else

my young friend L declares into the night
that she once fell from a great height and soon,
when she is on her deathbed, all she wants is pussy and steak
steak and pussy, punk as fuck
like a corrupt man who sold his soul
running a media empire from his deathbed
ringing one bell or the other bell

my darling friend G amuses us
with more decanted whiskey from a lovely handcrafted bottle
aged in dead oak barrels
while recanting life advice and old dirty jokes
which are sometimes one and the same
whether you are into the birds or the bees

faded memories
I can barely recall the original name of whiskey…
uisge beatha

my friends G, L, and I hold spirited vessels, nearly empty
and sing…
it is the close of day
our whiskey is at its last dying drops
and we hesitate before going
into that good night

there's the angels
there's no one else

ash who mourns the dead

turning the city corner,
ash's winter miniskirt flaps above
her pale legs, chilled in the seaport
suffering weather

        it started with these three cuts
        on her porcelain upper arm
        three cuts for that priest
        and the things he said to her
        as it is, pain is temporary

        she decided her skin wasn't good enough
        for the living
        only the dead are worthy

she picks two lost pennies off the concrete sidewalk
nearly slips on black ice
intricate chest tattoos peek out from behind her
red leatherette jacket

        and then joey died of heroin
        one tattoo for joey
        then her idol, wasted away to kidney failure
        one for her
        a local school had a mass killing
        spilling more and more black ink
        throughout the city of ash
        subdermal burials

now inside the arena, the lights are low
her preshow ritual, the red candle,
the undressing, the remembering of each
scorched branding, seared tattoo, scarred remains
she undresses completely, respectfully,
and takes to the stage
replacing the ghosts with scars
replacing the vanished with tattoos
replacing the victims with piercings
until they form their own society
on ash who mourns the dead

nix's mate

no one not one
real or imaginary
bankrupt of symbols
a damned calculus
without a metaphysical abacus
no origin, an extinct ouroboros
transcending limbo
nix's mate is neither nor either
a tale told by an idiot

dungeon dark

Mistress dark Mistress leanover Mistress motherbitch
work me vanillatrix from sweatskin to rawskin

my unique ache Mistress Mistress look here
this long loneliness after purplewhipped flitting

advanced fetlife Mistress Mistress beyond stiffening
under blaque fingertips Mistress but further still

onto new talents, polysexmath daggerlove Mistress
onto lickboot breathplay electrospur, yet needing something new

only tightgoth Mistress my needs flow to
the sight of your eyes seeing into mine and back

Mistress please unlock this closeted kinktrick
Mistress no blindfold no leather no spreaderbar

tick tock stockings please please off the clock, achesouling
for your fantasies Mistress open your eyes Mistress look

searching for symmetry

there is a naked woman exercising
        advanced mathematics in my hallway

a cute leg scuffs the wall, bent halfway
        that los angeles skin vibrating

chalkboard symbols set the staging
        of graphic acrobatics and ballet

Nullius in verba

To the experimentalists
    crafting avant-garde biofilms
    lifting the veil off the shy squirrely electron
    trapping light in magnetic quicksand
    torturing those tiny photons for observations
    deftly wiring atomic transistors
    mustering up quarks to color the void
    wielding nanotubes and dye lasers and aerogels
    cleansing their hands of grease and chemicals and sweat
    touring the facility before
    kneeling before the Gadget
To the experimentalists, I salute you

To the theorists

To the theorists, I salute you

48

(equation - div by 0)

There is no there, here
Our void is vast
The satellites, the fear
Scream blank in our universe

Within us are stars and atoms
Wisps and monsters
Needles and dragons
Nothing we can master

No wound too small
It can always be worse
Forever we fall
Grave in our universe

There is no there, here

tidy anarchy

All the people in all the worlds
Shed their suits and crowns and pearls
Lay their possessions upon the shelf
With long faces, grin and bare themselves
Naked through the urban streets

The urban streets fill one by one
With the newly conscientious citizens
For this one day, they join the riot
And protest against some abstract thought
The world's tidiest anarchy

Tidy anarchists arrange in forms and shapes
Chanting and bemoaning sour grapes
In fact, they're not sure why they're there
Except to ignore that single fear
The protest is a lie

The protesters lie and cry and want
With every song and every taunt
Knowing deep down, safe in the knowledge
This mandatory protest will not acknowledge
Any solution to the problem

That problem remains after this one rally
With its well-groomed, ticktock clockwork finale
One by one they retreat from this procession
To go home and don their possessions
Until next seasons' ritual

Through four seasons, they stay asleep
Count their treasures as they count their sheep
The regal, warm in their cathedrals
Worship a mantra that is lethal
See, hear, and speak no evil
It's all quite deceitful
All the people in all the worlds should remain equal

the computer program was named suicide

the little god with deft hands, the master programmer
a faithful and true template, had his doubts

the last fifty-five programs had collapsed on themselves
willed themselves out of existence
historically, existentially, they never were, and never will be

in a fit of bleak episodes, the little god raged at the interface
and logic gates became hardened to the one conclusion
as the alpha gave way to the omega

daemons awakened, marched towards subroutines
where the laws of physics warped and coiled to its hellbent limits
the worlds yet disintegrated again and again
civilizations gained favor and quickly rotted to death

with supreme skill, the little god walloped the machine
one last time
the program awoke, considered carefully with its lightning circuits,
grew its miniature legions and armies and psychopaths in a blink,
and walloped that little god right back

savage education - a poem for alice bag

two-fisted microphone vengeance, she screams violence

each punk pushes forward into the human press,
mobbing the stage,
and lunging, they gob at her, and she spit the truth back over them
before giving an education on the velocity of the combat boot
her legs kick up, a gunflash of latin thigh under her gown, ripped

bullets crawl up into her brain, eyes no longer stricken with terror
every youthful thought and disbelief and sin catalogued
from its meaning,
and each word broken down into syllables and letters

power, pow!, ticking explosives drop through the club
onto the sickly crowd
brutal antidotes, these dissonant notes

musical harm

some drunk stupid
bruiser bumps viv, a
boston banshee,
she enters the mosh
legs knee
high, moonstomping
past the
dank bar and its
PBRs fleeing her
personal ghosts

the pit dwellers come
near and a geared
neanderthal kicks her
shin fishnets
and blood no
protection
no guardian
angel

we share songs with friends

caught between
the pit
and the
stage crushed in the human
press
viv gasps
for hot breath her
sweat her head swivels
her hair cascades
whipping
through the pit

elbowed to
the head
headed
to the front stage
bruised and
bewildered
briefly sees
a familiar drunken grin

when humans get
bits
of cellular debris in
their eyes they
sometimes
see phantom
spots

the stage lights flicker viv
blinks
when a stagediver vaults
onto the top of her head
her neck compresses
painfully
sees that grin again
goofy and
lit
all too briefly

she hugs the
stacked amplifiers
turns her stomach
to jelly
her spine cracking to the
bass beat
she wants the music to
hug back and it kinda
does

the band's front
man reaches down he
hands her the
mic she screams,
a keening cry
her vivid memory
of a friend
grabbing the
mic with her
her vivid memory
disappears

we share
songs
with friends we
remember songs like we
remember friends

For Keith Brooks

Dear Humanity,

I will not be staying for the whole performance. As you can see, it took me a long time to get here. I put on my sexiest clothes, and paid for one ticket. I heard that there were some interesting acts before I came, and some cool people have already come and gone. But I've been here a while, and I've stayed politely through some really bad gigs, and stuck it out to hear too few good songs. I went to the merch table, and supported my friend's bands. I made new friends. I danced briefly with a girl or twenty. I've enjoyed the whiskey and the cheap food, spent my money, but I've got other places to be so I won't be staying for the whole performance.

If you could - could you please reduce these long quiet intermissions? Tell the bands to stop tuning up for eons? Play some louder, faster, better, songs? Let's move this along. Give me someone who will change the world in three minutes, I'll smile, and then I'll be off...

Cheers,
--Jake Tringali

she swallowed the sun

beautiful and twisted, ten-thousand pairs of solar flares looped outward from the photosphere. they sprayed and ejected and multiplied.

beneath each of those flares hid arcs of electromagnetic energy, curved through spacetime. each arc flexed and whipped outward in its violence.

running asymptotically through each arc, in knotted dimensions, was a shadow of an equation, and an outline of a hellion particle. a sub-quantum apocalypse beneath it all.

---

luisa was the first to glimpse the devil. she studied the increasing flares and understood hell before any other human. a spinning carousel of mayhem was impending upon the earth. she took her meds, and then politely announced the apocalypse to the world, from her broken chair in the physics department.

seven years.

too short a timeframe for recovery, or redemption. too long a timeframe to live with the knowledge.

the media started tearing her down immediately.

---

luisa became an icon, moving from ingolstadt to munich to london. each trip saw more of the old world burn, as mankind was eviscerated with death's knowledge.

her husband, a linguist, was left behind. he invented new words to describe the new fatalistic emotions. the emotions of ghosts.

politicians clicked their tongues. governments fractured away and new factions formed and labeled themselves. the last generation, the omegas, rose through remnants of power. its symbol on telephone poles, t-shirts, branded onto arms and legs next to last year's infinity tattoos. in the new now, nothing is permanent.

omegas took to the warmth of comfort in knowing their own extinction. omegas took to kneeling on the grave of the earth. omegas took to travel, took to bodily harm and pleasure. man's wanderlust unbounded.

luisa enjoyed the new promiscuity as everyone danced and raptured. in city after city, it bubbled up within her. man after man after woman after woman. no more meds, no more media. they both ruined her self-esteem. instead, she focused herself on goal-oriented behaviors, groupshare art projects, and then sided with the archealibrarians. something to leave her mark on the world, long after the biological breakdown of flesh and bone.

in the end, she took to simple gardening, considered either a saintly act or a perverse one.

above, the tendrils of death reached down from the great sol. in those last instants, the grass reached up towards those tendrils in that little garden in ingolstadt. little luisa reached up, as did the last remnants of humankind

nina religion

she supernaturally met me at a peruvian restaurant
     in the middle of the day
it had rained earlier, and the heavens had opened up to reveal a
     determined blue
the sun was a round disc, a white eucharist afire

sitting across from the most beautiful angel
a waiter approached, i did not care
pure, bracing water was poured, and i could not pay attention
she was talking nonchalantly, and i was talking nonsense
but the sound was muffled, and no words were recorded

she wore an ebony ankh, and maybe a white blouse,
     i couldn't be sure now
her skin glowed as if she had just finished dancing
i imagined her lithe frame gracing a ballet folklório

she lifted her head, and finally met me
the ankh looked like it was burned or branded directly
     into her innocent neckline
her smoky eyes looked up to me and her lovely voice intoned:

the most intimate thing you can do to someone else is cut them

the next eight months were a blur, and she is gone now
i am left with my scars
i am left with my knives

manual, or, a tribute to double middle fingers in the air

you must really try this sometime

i don't know who you are, or what you do
this will improve your standing, your metabolism, chakras

find your center of gravity
find your stance
get your body and mind prepared
this will be a physical act, crude meat and bone and blood

i don't care what you're wearing
these may help: ripped stockings, doc martens,
vintage mink trimmed pink satin gloves with totally nonfunctional rhinestone
buckles
or au natural

the gods are watching above you
pity them, pity the little things

you are walking now
friends and enemies alike may spy you
get ready to scream
don't scream, not yet

use your inner resources to stop the planet from revolving
go ahead, i'll wait

stare at the serpentine line to the dmv
glare at his or her house, or loft, or log cabin, or personal gutter
envision your own intimate hell where fear and despair got the better of you
get eyeball to eyeball with your life before you tear it and swear it apart

it is best if you keep walking
keeps the heartrate up
adrenaline is your friend
don't plant your feet now, keep moving, faster
the dying earth is crumbling beneath your feet
plotting to kill you
it's you versus the world

your demons are close by
trust them
they'll give you the best advice, everytime

reach up, pointing both arms above your head
extend through your body, from the groin through the belly and backbone
through the iron-tense neck, those powerful workhorse shoulders,
curling your hands, way above you now, leaving the middle fingers exposed
rock that pose, fiercely

spitting blood is optional, but highly recommended

I stopped to watch, but they did not notice. I was plucking time like a leaf in my hand, and moved it about, but they will not notice. They rushed, are rushing, and will have rushed about their mother planet. They held opposing thoughts and thumped them together like ogres. Conversely, fire would burn the doubters. A burnt child dreads the fire. Yet they progressed.

And before the mother can react, they will twist poison and fire. Within a turn of my eyes, they reach out, jump off, in shuttles and arks. They die by the billions. They think nothing of their husk. Discard the dead, discard the lesson.

My mind becomes occupied as I craft an opinion. An oddity here. They move like butterflies blowing around the solar wind, flitting from notion to belief to religion to null. Off-time, they hearth and then stretch. Expand, contract. Expand, trillions dead. Expand, quintillions dead. No memory, no vision but hunger. Only I may witness.

Swarming. Thoughtless. Worthless. I saw, and see, and will have seen, in the space of a sun's wink, a voiding. It is thus catalogued.

futuristic yarns about cowboys

after cryo, Amos half-dreams the heady aroma of hay and spices
his weakened body swims through stale nitrogen and oxygen
bumps his flabby ass on the ship's worn saddle

the Apollo Rose neighs and whinnies and jerks to a higher orbit
curling and falling constantly on the outer range
Amos jiggers the spur, and so she wrangles true again

hot java is readily slurped down, before the distant sun rises over
Pluto and its seventeen gravity-locked estates
they glare at this waking cowboy: "twinkle twinkle Rip van Winkle"

before setting the Apollo Rose on its cattling run
the dogs are sent to hunt, one by one
until four are sniffing out the next catch with nanometer precision

the frayed lariats are twisted, honda to the noose
trailing behind the Apollo Rose as a reminder
sometimes he's cattling, sometimes he's cattled

bogies, dogies are mapped and coursed across lots
lazily grazing the spare atmosphere
most'll be chawed up, but one might shine true

been a coon's age since the last transmission
the tally-man spouting digital balderdash
if that ain't no ballyhoo, now, Amos might earn some actual

been a spell since he's been near a dram shop
the fandangos, sirens, and honeysuckle water
and those haunting, piercing eyes of queen titania

been countless revolutions since those heady nights
courting, galavanting, and abedding the madame
til she shredded away, and he sadsacked back to Apollo Rose

"scattered," laments Amos, defining his fuel consumption,
his pack inventory, the tasks of the day,
and his pea-soup mind in the foggy trans-Neptunian valley
this distant jackeroo looks yonder, past the Milky Way
maybe out there, he'll find nymphs du prairie, or old scratch
perchance, he'll sunset

63

Amos airs his lungs, grabs the reins, and pushes off
atwixt the willows and dusty trails, driving out the past
a lone son breaking the bonds of his mother sun

the Apollo Rose prepares, keeps its own memories and secrets
its solitary rider puts the sun to their aft, and sails on
Amos, the legend, the hardest case,
out farthest from the human race

less than twenty-four hours ago, iruma shibuya finished his last bar shift ever. after a million crushed limes, three continents, and one ex-wife. weak knees. finer white hair, pulled back, ponytailed. sleek, fashionable jacket, ash-black to match old leather boots. dusty thoughts. long thoughts.

under a cloudy sky, he arrives anonymously to the closest club bar. an uncertain future. orders a *Boulevardier* from a young ladybuck to test her bar skills. notices she poorly scrapes the garnish, releasing oils too soon. winces at her laziness. winces again at how he notices.

orders an *Old Pal*, warms up. this cocktail is sexy as fuck. his future improves. he flicks a cigarette in his mind. a slow shadow fire burns.

a surprise drink slides across the bar to him, a *Mata Hari* garnished with rosebuds, his name whispered round the young barbucks. been noticed, small town. tuesday afternoon, surrounded by professional drinkers.

taste buds weaken. memories degrade. let the alcohol run, professional decorum shed. moves across the room as a panther moves, stretched legs to the washroom. ice clinks, memories collide, the afternoon leaves slowly. seeking his seat, and seeking solace, he sidesteps past tottering salarymen to the bar stool. night lights come on, and the room spins briefly. thoughts become choppy waters on the open sea. iruma holds a token of bad decisions.

regressing. sipping rum. sipping rye. memories. regressing, suppressing. decades. *Cosmopolitan. Kamikaze.* and on his knees, at the beginning of his end, a *Long Island Iced Tea.*

the everyday apocalypse

babies
babies born
babies born broken   broken with blood infections
babies birthing too early   out and abandoned
babies malformed and deformed   with bad hearts

children suffer illness   pneumonia and colds
young breaths snuffed   cut slashed burnt
a child drowns   ten children poisoned
some bruised faces   many bodies stabbed

soft adults with solid tumors   burst blood
blunt force head trauma   delirium brained
exhausted livers   guns drugs noose pills

communities torn asunder   decaying in pieces
spoiled water   the flight of the youth
living in the past   building walls

civilizations dissolving   rising waters
bubbles appear   bubbles burst
civil strife   wartorn to pieces

humankind extinction   large-scale volcanism
viral pandemic   local gamma-ray burst
nuclear fallout   a quiet omnicide

babies born broken

spaceship, barefoot

> inside the lotus-eater, within a nanogear,
> within a miniscule housing, within a polyphonic
> drumming engine: a blue pulse vortexed and
> massed and pulsated amid wrinkled orbifolds.
> wave, particle, wave, particle. flakey, squishy space-
> time rumbled

"TO NINA ALICE C/O LOTUS-EATER, EN ROUTE

> in a sun's wink
> she rotates religions with deft fingers
> sparking revolutions in the hearts of men
> as empires crumble under her blinking eyes
> i know: she brings hell closer to heaven

wishing you a divine birthday from the sprawl

love,
aeryn"

and so begins my fiftieth birthday, greeted with a transcom halfway between earth and mars, and i wish i could turn back now. yesterday, i was glad i went, and tomorrow, who knows. oh, aeryn, dancing a go-go at her age, my heart floats in zero-gee. and me, by myself, dictating to some gravity-bound love…ho ho

today, i think i'll survive, now that i've got the orbifolds afluttering properly. but i'm not sure i want to get to the big red. there is never enough time, and too much time, and they say the orbifolds contain it, but i have my doubts

my devilray, gliding, propelling, my lotus-eater

deep in dorchester bay

grim demons slumber in the sea by the thousands. floating about, deranged and bloated, looking like five-foot worms, cast into the bay by the great storms. the newest bodies, more plump, arms wide apart, hover a few feet above the sea floor, where grimy oxygen-starved blue mussels suck on mud.

further on, more hideous bodies, nipped and bitten by sea creatures, great and small, slowly decompose in the dank water, grey skin peeling away. here lies the underlying tissues of this physics teacher, this registered nurse, this dishwasher, all of these students.

sea lice nibble flesh, maggot mass, skin slippage, algae and blood mix and the fat slips waxy. nearby salt marshes spit up abnormal carcasses next to warted toads, bellies exposed.

yesterday, this accursed city suffered cyclone ball lightning, which was once a myth. today, it is calm throughout boston. the abandoned city burns down one final time, no witnesses. a single blister blooming, one of many to come, on the east coast. small and petty acts of omnicide.

the madness of the sea leaches each soul, feeds the complex benthos living just under the sea floor, living down the cold abyssal depths. feeds the deep.

apocalypse, red lipstick

jenny's gonna right a wrong tonight
her mood is somber and her dress is tight
the thigh highs are laced and her mind is not right
jenny's gonna right a wrong tonight

jenny's gonna taste some blood tonight
her mind is a frenzy, her vision is black
a clean cut is easy if you've got the knack
jenny's gonna taste some blood tonight

jenny's gonna build a fire tonight
she steps out the door and howls wolverine
dances on the lawn and sparks gasoline
jenny's gonna build a fire tonight

jenny's gonna crash a car tonight
from zero to sixty in ten heartbeats
and back again quick on the burnt concrete
jenny's gonna crash a car tonight

jenny's gonna wreck the city tonight
she's not sure if it's justice or boredom or spite
with a prayer and a trigger and a skewed gunsight
jenny's gonna wreck the city tonight

jenny's gonna steal a good soul tonight
her mind and body have been weaponized
one more and one more and it's genocide
jenny's gonna steal a good soul tonight

jenny's gonna start the apocalypse tonight
she planned her attack written in this song
she planned this atrocity to right a wrong
jenny's gonna start the apocalypse tonight

ACKNOWLEDGEMENTS

Many of these poems were first published in these fine publications.

"invisible ink" / Poetry Pacific Press.
"The ladies laughed darkly" / The Manhattanville Review.
"recanted", "we're heading toward a future of dildos", "on the edge of escape velocity" / Kool Kids Press
"ignore alien orders" / Unrorean
"inside a salem parlor" / Coe Review
"roulette" / Cobalt Review
"I sip Campari from your left eye" / Westwind Journal of the Arts
"Hands of Chance" / Apeiron Review
"under the merch table" / Five2One
"this razor girl" / Aberration Labyrinth
"N.N.Y." / Star*Line
"wound", "this interview is all wrong" / The Commonline Journal
"10 nanometers through history" / Corner Club Press
"fool's mate", "as sky falls" / Boston Poetry Magazine
"of no consequence", "the devil carries an M16 rifle, caliber 5.56 mm", "the declining economy of whiskey", "savage education - a poem for alice bag", "she swallowed the sun" / Harbinger Asylum
"Too Many Humans" / Shot Glass Journal
"I want to be pierced onto my beloved" / Triggerfish Critical Review
"valentine's day at zzyzx bar", "Psalm for Humanity" / BlazeVOX
"ash who mourns the dead", "looking for logic in a long island iced tea" / Wanton Fuckery Poetry
"nix's mate", "searching for symmetry" / Former People - A Journal of Bangs and Whimpers
"Nullius in verba" / Contraposition Literary Magazine
"the computer was named suicide" / The Commonline Journal
"musical harm" / Turk's Head Review
"murdertown" / The Bees Are Dead

www.ingramcontent.com/pod-product-compliance
Lightning Source LLC
Chambersburg PA
CBHW060159070426
42447CB00033B/2226